THE G.I. SERIES

The Georgia Hussars were one of many Southern militia companies that wore distinctive uniforms. Hailing from Savannah, Georgia, the company had adopted the uniform prior to the war. They raised two companies for the war; Company A, Georgia Hussars became Company F of the Jeff Davis Legion and Company B, Georgia Hussars served as Company D, 2nd Battalion Georgia Cavalry.

THE G. I. SERIES

THE ILLUSTRATED HISTORY OF THE AMERICAN SOLDIER, HIS UNIFORM AND HIS EQUIPMENT

Johnny Reb
The Uniform of the Confederate Army 1861–1865

Leslie D. Jensen

CHELSEA HOUSE PUBLISHERS
PHILADELPHIA

First Chelsea House hardback edition published 2000.

Library of Congress Cataloging-in-Publication Data
Jensen, Les.
Johnny Reb: the uniform of the Confederate Army, 1861–1865 / Leslie D. Jensen.
   p.   cm. — (The G.I. series)
Originally published: London: Greenhill Books; Mechanicsburg, Pa., USA: Stackpole Books, © 1996, in series: The G.I. series; 5.
Includes index.
Summary: Describes the uniforms worn by members of the Confederate Army during the Civil War.
ISBN 0-7910-5369-5 (hc.)
1. Confederate States of America. Army—Uniforms.
[1. Confederate States of America. Army—Uniforms.]
I. Title.   II. Series: G.I. series (Philadelphia, Pa.)
UC483.5.J46 1999
355.1'4'097309034—dc21

                                        99-21375
                                          CIP

ACKNOWLEDGEMENTS
In addition to the various institutions who have provided images for this publication the author wishes especially to thank Robin Reed, Melinda Collier, Guy Swanson, Bill Turner, Dave Mark, J. Luther Sowers, Michael J. McAfee, Adam Dintenfass, Michael J. Black, Herb Peck, Bill Moore, Michael Kramer, Harris Andrews, Nicky Hughes, Tom Fugate, Michael J. Winey, Randy Hackenberg, Bill Frassanito, Pat Schroeder, Ron Sheetz, Michael J. Vice, Eleanor F. Hewlett, and Juanita Leisch.

ABBREVIATIONS

MOC	Eleanor S. Brockenbrough Library, Museum of the Confederacy, Richmond, VA
GHM	Greensboro Historical Museum, Greensboro, NC
NA	National Archives
LC	Library of Congress, Washington, DC
CV	Confederate Veteran Magazine
Mass MOLLUS	Massachusetts Commandery, Military Order of the Loyal Legion of the United States, housed at the U.S. Army Military History Institute, Carlisle Barracks, PA

Photographs without sources are from private collections whose owners wish to remain anonymous.

PUBLISHER'S NOTE
While many Confederate soldiers might have rebelled against being referred to as 'G.I.s', they none the less were American soldiers, who happened to be engaged in fighting other American soldiers. In this light, the present volume has been included in this series. Also note that certain terms used in this publication relative to 'Richmond Depot Type I, II and III' jackets are modern designations based on the author's considerable research of the rare existing images and uniform specimens. They are not terms of the 1860s. The author uses these terms to help clarify different types of uniforms for the reader, and to encourage further research in this very difficult field.

Designed and edited by DAG Publications Ltd
Designed by David Gibbons
Layout by Anthony A. Evans
Printed in Hong Kong

JOHNNY REB:
THE UNIFORM OF THE CONFEDERATE ARMY
1861–1865

he secession of South Carolina from the United ̣ates of America on 20 December 1860, in ̣sponse to the election of Abraham Lincoln as ̣esident, ended 40 years of rivalry and debate ̣tween the Northern and Southern states over con-̣itutional issues, the rights of states versus the ̣deral government, and the institution of slavery. ̣ather than remain in a Union now dominated by ̣nti-slavery forces, South Carolina, followed by ̣labama, Georgia, Mississippi, Florida, Louisiana ̣nd Texas, acted on their long-standing assertion ̣at as sovereign states voluntarily in the Union, ̣ey could at any time withdraw.

When these states formed the Confederate States ̣f America in March, 1861, they hoped the break ̣ith the Federal Union could be made peacefully. ̣evertheless, on 6 March 1861, the Confederacy ̣stablished its own regular army, a force of roughly ̣,000 men, followed by an authorization for a Pro-̣isional Army of the Confederate States, enlisted ̣r one year, to be made up of 100,000 volunteers ̣rovided by the states.

Although most Federal Army posts in the South ̣ere evacuated peacefully, at Charleston, South ̣arolina, the Federal garrison refused to leave. ̣stead, it moved to the island fortification of Fort ̣umter, squarely blockading the harbor entrance. ̣he Confederacy could not allow such foreign ̣roops to stay on Confederate soil and still remain ̣ viable nation. Thus, within a few weeks of the ̣ation's establishment, a military solution was to be ̣pplied to a diplomatic problem. From then on, the ̣onfederacy's story became largely a military one. ̣ltimately, the nation lasted only so long as its ̣rmy.

South Carolina troops stepped up pressure on ̣he garrison while fruitless negotiations dragged on ̣ith Washington over Fort Sumter's fate. At last, ̣onfederate patience wore out. At 4:30 a.m, on 12 ̣pril 1861, South Carolina batteries opened fire, ̣ombarding Sumter until it surrendered late the ̣ext day.

Federal response was immediate. Lincoln called ̣or 75,000 militia to put down the rebellion. In response, North Carolina, Tennessee, Arkansas and Virginia seceded and joined the Confederacy. In Maryland, Kentucky and Missouri, pro-Southern factions passed secession ordinances or contributed troops to the Confederacy but quick Federal occupation put an end to any effective secession movement. In May, the Confederate capital was moved to Richmond, Virginia, a mere 110 miles from Washington, DC.

The close distance between the two capitals, the Confederacy's 3,000 mile-coastline, and the Mississippi River's bisection of the new nation were the geographic facts that dictated the course of the war. Early on, Lincoln approved the so-called Anaconda Plan. It was intended to strangle the Confederacy by a blockade of the coast, followed by cutting it in two along the Mississippi, with later moves inland. Through it all, the capture of Richmond remained a prime Federal objective.

To maintain its sovereignty, the Confederacy had only to survive. Confederate strategy was essentially defensive; to keep as much territory as possible, and to invade the North as opportunities offered to force peace. Mainly, they hoped to wear the Federals down and force them to give up the invasion. The Federals, on the other hand, had to invade and conquer in order to re-establish Federal power in the South. As a result, the war was fought largely on Southern soil. This fact had much to do with the way the Confederate Army, strategically, tactically and spiritually, fought the war.

Although the Confederate Army existed for only four short years, during that time it established a reputation as one of the finest fighting forces the world has seen. There are a number of reasons for this. First, the army was highly motivated because its soil was being invaded and families, homes and firesides were in imminent danger. As Federal invasions resulted in burned homes, displaced families and lost property, this reaction only became stronger. For Southerners, the war was a second American revolution, fought, like the first, to rid themselves of an oppressive government. The more the Federals prosecuted the war, the more Yankees became not merely former fellow citizens on a wrong course, but foreigners representing a despotic dictator. Moreover, the threat to slavery, the economic basis of the Southern economy and a basic fact behind the Southern social order, produced a reaction that was almost neurotic in its extremes. Thus, on one level, the war was about constitutional and legal issues; on another, it was over defending homes and firesides; and on a third, it was at a gut level that was explainable only if one had actually lived in that place and time. By the midpoint of the war, reconciliation with the Federals was impossible and the Confederate Army fought because it was now a war to the death.

A second reason why the Confederate Army did so well was its officer corps. Many were graduates of the U.S. Military Academy at West Point, and connected to Southern aristocracy; they were used to responsibility and command. Although the number of West Pointers in the Confederate Army was limited (only about a third of the Regular Army's officers joined the Southern cause), there were enough of them to command many divisions and brigades and almost all the field armies, and to occupy all the full general positions. Many other Confederate officers, often down to company level, were graduates of Southern military schools, while others had come from some form of responsible position in civil life, either as plantation owners, politicians, professors or the like.

Basic organization had much to do with the army's resilience and toughness. Volunteer companies were recruited locally. Thus, the men already knew one another, many were inter-related, and all had personal reputations to uphold if they expected to be able to return home when the war ended. Even the majority of conscripts, who entered the army after a draft was instituted in 1862, came from the same areas as the units they joined. Most Confederate armies placed regiments from the same state in brigades, and thus there grew up strong state-oriented unit pride and esprit.

Perhaps the most important factor in the Confederate Army's success as a fighting force, however, was the quality of the men themselves. They were largely young, enthusiastic and spoiling for a fight. Early in the war, their motto was 'one Rebel can lick ten Yankees', and they truly believed it. Although experience showed that the Federals were a potent foe, most Confederates, deep down, believed in ultimate victory. Because they were young, and for many, away from home for the first time, the war was a great adventure. This, plus a strong sense of humor, kept up spirits to the end. Just as important, their families were as a rule strongly supportive. Many a wife told her soldier husband not to come back except under honorable circumstances; and many civilians, as individuals and in soldiers' aid societies, contributed greatly to

a feeling among Confederates that the people were behind them.

As the war dragged on and increasing defeat caused this confidence to be shaken, it was to a certain extent replaced by religious conviction. The great revival movements in the Confederate armies in 1864 and 1865 reinforced the fighting spirit by giving the men a strong set of beliefs that the cause was right, just and blessed by the Lord. Thus Confederates had a strong set of spiritual reserves to draw upon to keep their confidence alive, and that confidence proved a potent factor in making them tough and dependable fighters.

Still, it took some time for these advantages to take hold. The Confederate Regular Army never reached full strength and was essentially a cipher in the war; and the volunteers were handicapped by their resistance to Regular Army discipline. At first regular procedure was followed only until it became boring, and basic drill was only partially learned. Though there were some good officers, many had little real knowledge of what to do. They tended to command by persuasion and friendliness, and their units were sometimes out of control.

The first battles brought a dose of reality, but not until 1862 did most Confederate armies begin to take on real discipline. This was due in part to the conscription act, passed early that year, which changed the basic relationship between the soldier and the government. Under its terms, the one-year volunteers, whose terms all expired in the spring of 1862, were given a choice; they could re-enlist for the duration of the war, and would be granted a furlough, a chance to change commands and the right to elect new officers. If they did not re-enlist, they would be drafted with no choices. At one stroke, the Confederate Army was no longer a volunteer army, but a drafted one. Although this caused some dissension and resentment in the ranks, it also brought home the seriousness of the war. Most men accepted these new terms as a harsh necessity and soldiered on, their ardor for the cause undampened.

One unfortunate result of the law was the election of new officers. In many companies, the officers had begun to impose hard discipline. Now many men rid themselves of these martinets and elected more easy-going officers. This led to a high degree of military disorganization, and caused the Confederate Army to enter the battles of 1862 almost as a new force. Many of these new officers lasted only a few months, whereas those that stayed generally tended to learn their duties and become more effective.

On the positive side, this new force was in the hands of general officers who imposed stronger discipline. General Braxton Bragg, much vilified for his tactical errors and personality problems, was nonetheless an excellent organizer and disciplinarian

1. The western armies began to see regular inspec-
ons, punishments and uniformly applied doctrine
d drill. These standards augured well in keeping
em together and functioning in later years despite
feat after defeat.

For many Confederate commanders, the most
orrisome problem was straggling. Men who could
ot be kept in ranks on the march reduced the
my's strength, and in battle, every man counted.
us, men such as General Thomas J. 'Stonewall'
ckson enforced strict march discipline. He
posed a schedule of marching fifty minutes and
sting ten, and insisted that the ranks be kept well
osed up. When General A. P. Hill was late getting
s troops on the road, Jackson had him court-mar-
led. His methods were harsh and one captured
onfederate exclaimed, 'All Old Jack ever gave us
as a blanket and forty rounds, and he druv us like
ll.' Still, Jackson's methods brought his men vic-
ries, and they became willing to follow him any-
here.

The greatest Confederate commander, Robert E.
e, was at first regarded merely as an old staff offi-
r with no real record of success. But after the
ring of victories from the Seven Days to Chancel-
rsville, Lee's Army of Northern Virginia possessed
ch confidence that when they invaded Pennsylva-
a in the early summer of 1863, many fully
lieved their ultimate destination to be Baltimore,
iladelphia or New York, where they would dictate
ace and end the war. Their defeat at Gettysburg,
hile a hard blow, did not cripple them, and they
mained a tough foe for two more years before the
d came. Through it all, their confidence in Robert
Lee never faltered. Indeed, one young officer told
e in the last days of the war, 'You are the Confed-
acy, General, it is you that they fight for.'

Because the Confederate Army was a fighting
my, made up of citizen soldiers whose sole pur-
ose was to finish the war and go home, it never
eveloped a tradition or love for military display
d pageantry in the manner of other armies.
deed, it would have been anathema to those
emocratic individualists who made up the army.
hough they learned proper drill, tactics and disci-
line, they did so only to win victory in battle; any-
ing that did not lead to that end was quickly
ropped.

The Confederate Regular Army did not have uni-
orm regulations until June 1861. Before that, Reg-
lar Army recruits were clothed in gray trousers,
d or white flannel shirts and a blue fatigue blouse,
ut no cap. Uniform regulations were issued on 6
ne 1861. The best evidence is that the uniform
as designed by Nicola Marschall, an Austrian artist
ving in Montgomery, Alabama, then the Confeder-
cy's capital. Marschall's inspiration were some
ustrian *jägers* he had seen in 1859, and the uni-
orm bears a strong resemblance to Austrian uni-

forms of the period. Although very few, if any, of
these uniforms were made for enlisted men, the
regulations became the standard for Confederate
officers, both regular and volunteer. They also
inspired several state regulations.

The Confederacy's initial policy on uniforming
troops was simple; the Regular Army would be uniformed by the government, while the volunteers
would provide their own uniforms, and be paid for
the expense by the government. This was the Commutation System, a typical American policy that had
been used in other wars. It kept the government out
of the uniform-manufacturing business, and provided a simple way of shifting the burden of clothing the troops to the states and local communities.

When the war began, some of the older volunteer
companies were already uniformed in resplendent
outfits. These uniforms were typical of American
volunteer militia in general, and had no particular
regional style. In the late 1850s, many units had
adopted a version of the U.S. Regular Army dress in
response to state laws which prescribed such a uniform. Other organizations had uniforms unique to
themselves, but often copied from the 7th New
York, then the trend-setter in militia garb. A few
units, mainly in the large cities, adopted Zouave
dress, but the Zouave movement was never as popular in the South as in the North. None of these uniforms lasted in active service more than a few
months.

The new volunteer companies tended to adopt
either gray or blue frock coats or jackets, although
a significant number of companies entered the war
in variously trimmed overshirts, and without coats.
A few states actually issued uniforms to their
troops. North Carolina supplied a loose sack coat
with a six-button front and sewed-down shoulder
straps in the branch color, gray trousers, and a gray
felt hat. Georgia supplied gray frock coats, and both
states adopted black, rather than sky-blue, as the
infantry color. Mississippi developed a modified
rank system, prescribed frock coats with herring-
bone trim on the front, and designated red as the
infantry color. However, while it prescribed uniforms, Mississippi actually issued only buttons.
Mississippi troops either followed or ignored the
state regulations and when they were followed,
there was considerable variation in interpretation.

By summer 1861, reports were coming into Richmond of ragged Confederates in the field. Many volunteers had worn uniforms of substandard goods,
which quickly wore out. Now, hundreds of miles
from home, they had no easy way to replenish the
supply, and in many areas of the South, the cloth
market had dried up. Faced with this situation, the
Confederate quartermaster's department began to
issue clothing to volunteers in need.

To do so, it set up clothing manufacturing facili-
ties, first in Richmond, and later in other Southern

cities as well. These 'clothing depots' were modeled on the U.S. Army's facility at Schuylkill Arsenal, Philadelphia, Pennsylvania. The depots contracted with local mills for the cloth. Despite attempts at uniformity, the various mills had different capabilities and supplied varying types of cloth. Some made excellent all-wool material, but the majority supplied woolen jeans, a fabric made with a cotton warp and a woolen weft, often undyed or poorly dyed with substances that soon turned a light brown, or 'butternut' hue.

In time, the basic uniform evolved into a short jacket and trousers, and the uniform regulations, though still in force, had little bearing on the design of what was issued. Each depot tended to develop its own patterns and designs, and there was no central control over the actual look of the uniform.

The depot staffs were small, about 40 men on average. They cut out the uniforms, packaged and issued them, and kept the accounts. Large numbers of women in the cities did the actual sewing in their homes and were paid by the piece. Most depots employed between 2,000 and 3,000 seamstresses. With this force, the depots produced considerable quantities of uniforms. Atlanta, for example, turned out 40,000 jackets and trousers in 1863, while Richmond provided 150,000 uniforms the same year.

Agents were sent to England to contract for cloth, and this material began to arrive in 1863. The quality was excellent, and clothing made from this material was serviceable and warm. Despite the blockade, large amounts of English cloth found their way into the Confederacy. It may well be that the Confederate soldier was as well, or better, clothed in the latter part of the war than at the beginning.

This system was so successful that on 8 October 1862, the government officially ended the Commutation System and replaced it with an issue system, in which each soldier received certain specified items each year. If a soldier underdrew the clothing, he would be paid the value of the balance. If he overdrew, he had the amount taken out of his pay. Although it took some time for this system to be implemented fully, it was in general use in the main armies by 1863. Unfortunately, one veteran remembered that while the quantity usually met the regulation, the quality of the domestically made cloth was often poor, and the troops tended to wear out the clothing quickly. Thus, many troops were still ragged in the field and supplemented their government-issue clothing with items from home or captured Yankee uniforms. Indeed, the government even had a program for scouring and dyeing captured uniforms for issue, and it continued to solicit clothing from Ladies' Aid Societies and other sources.

Confederate quartermaster policy was that keeping the men clothed was always more important than keeping them uniformed. Given the variety sources for cloth in the issue clothing, as well as the various ways the basic uniform was supplemented, it is no surprise that the Confederate Army looked as if its men were wearing anything and everything. Even so, although variety certainly existed, the basic uniform designs are limited and easy to identify. Ultimately, the Confederacy's supply system was reasonably successful in meeting its first obligation to keep the troops clothed and warm.

In the final analysis, the Confederate Army was a fighting army. It concentrated on strategy and tactics, manpower strengths and winning the next battle. Uniforms, and particularly uniformity, were never very important. There is no evidence that the Confederacy lost the war because of a lack of clothing, but at the same time, in contrast to the days of Napoleon, uniforms had no particular effect on battles either. Still, the very sight of thousands of roughly clad rebels, screaming the rebel yell at the top of their lungs, unnerved Union troops. One Federal Major described the effect as follows:

'...who could fight such people? Indians! Worse than an Apache. Just as we would get into line of battle and ready for an advance, a little Georgia Colonel, in his shirt sleeves and copperas breeches would pop out into a corn field at the head of his regiment, and shout at the top of his voice "Charge!" Man alive! here would come the devils like a whirl-wind – over ditches, gullies, fences, and fields, shouting, yelling, whooping, that makes the cold chills run up your back – flash their glittering bayonets in our very faces, and break our line before you could say "boo!" Do you call that fighting? It was murder.'

FOR FURTHER READING

Freeman, Douglas Southall, *Lee's Lieutenants: Study in Command*, 4 vols., (New York: Charles Scribner's Sons, 1942–3)

Johnson, Robert Underwood and Clarence Clough Buel, eds., *Battles and Leaders of the Civil War*, vols., (New York: Thomas Yoseloff, 1956)

McCarthy, Carleton, *Detailed Minutiae of Soldier Life in the Army of Northern Virginia*, 1882, (Reprint New York: Time-Life Books, 1982)

Time-Life, et al, *Echoes of Glory*, (New York: Time Life Books, 1990)

Wiley, Bell Irvin, *The Life of Johnny Reb* (Baton Rouge: Louisiana State University Press, 1971)

olonel John S. Mosby, by Edward Caledon Bruce. One of the
w known wartime portraits of Confederate officers, Mosby
t for this painting in February 1865 in Richmond. He
ears a regulation double-breasted cavalry coat with yellow

collar and the stars of a colonel. His buttons are Confederate
staff and he carries a gray slouch hat with edge binding in
his hand. His cape, which appears to be dark gray or black,
with a black collar, is lined in red and may be civilian. (MOC)

Above: This postwar lithograph of the camp of the 3nd Kentucky Infantry near Corinth, Mississippi, in the late spring of 862 was done from a painting by Conrad Wise Chapman, who served in the regiment and sketched it from life. Chapman's roops have gray jackets and trousers, but most have shed them and appear in variously colored shirts and headgear. A variety of tentage is also seen, from wall tents and Sibley tents to shelters made of tree boughs.

Opposite page: A detail of Chapman's print of the 3rd Kentucky's camp shows a sergeant wearing sky-blue chevrons playing cards in the foreground. Note the red blanket. Judging from contemporary paintings, these were relatively common.

Left: This detail from Captain James Hope's *The Battle of Antietam* shows gun crews of Stephen D. Lee's artillery battalion firing at the Federals near the Dunker Church. Hope, who was an eyewitness to the battle, depicted the Confederates predominantly in brownish uniforms and shirts, a combination that other evidence supports for this period of the war. Only the officers appear to have gray uniforms, though some enlisted men have portions of them. (Antietam National Battlefield)

Opposite page, bottom: James Walker's painting of the Confederate attack on the first day at Gettysburg is an interesting mix of accurate details and apparent fabrication. The predominantly butternut uniforms and slouch hats are consistent with what is known of Confederate dress in the battle. Many of the troops in the background wear their blankets over their shoulders, a typical Confederate practice. On the other hand, those in the front, with a blanket roll at their backs hanging from a strap, reflect Walker's paintings of the Mexican War. Moreover, his use of battle streamers on the battle flags, also shown in his Mexican War paintings, are not known from any other source. (West Point Museum)

Below: Another detail from Walker's Gettysburg painting shows straw hats or slouch hats with feathers, both known Confederate practice. Here, the men wear knapsacks with blankets on top; another version of this painting shows the knapsacks as captured Federal pieces, with Federal regimental designations on them. Captured equipment was much in evidence among Confederates by 1863. The officer waving his sword is resplendent in his frock coat with sky blue collar, but inexplicably wears an artillery kepi. (West Point Museum).

Left: Conrad Wise Chapman's painting of a Confederate battery in Charleston, South Carolina, shows the crew reasonably well uniformed in brownish-gray clothing. One man wears sky-blue trousers. Charleston often had first chance at goods run through the blockade, and its troops were probably somewhat better clothed than those in the field. Chapman was an eyewitness to these scenes, was assigned by General Beauregard to sketch them, and later worked them into paintings. (MOC)

Opposite page: This painting, *Mosby's Command Attacking a Union Convoy Near Berryville*, was painted in 1868 by the French artist Paul Philippoteaux, who had been commissioned to do the work the year before by a Confederate veteran. His depiction of the landscape is reasonably accurate, and he shows Mosby's men uniformly in gray jackets (some with yellow collars), narrow brimmed, low-crown slouch hats and a mix of sky-blue and gray trousers, the sky-blue predominant. The troops are armed only with revolvers, a characteristic of Mosby's men. Though clearly in the romantic style, this painting is nearly contemporary to the war and probably is reasonably accurate. (MOC)

Below: Richard Norris Brooke painted *Furling the Flag* in 1872. His Confederates wear a mixture of clothing, the majority with gray trousers. Three enlisted men wear gray jackets in various styles. The drummer's has shoulder straps and belt loops. Most of the men wear only shirts, primarily white, while headgear is almost evenly divided between hats and caps. The officer with his arm in a sling is an artilleryman, while the man to his left may be from the staff. Two men are barefoot, but another has white leggings. Although unusual, they do occasionally appear in contemporary images. The canteen on the same man is clearly Federal. (West Point Museum)

Captain William J. Stores, Company I, 32nd Virginia Infantry. This ambrotype, taken in Richmond, is tinted ever so slightly in sky-blue on the collar and cuffs. Stores does not wear the prescribed sleeve braid, merely a pointed cuff. His trousers were probably dark blue.

ny Southern states,
their uniform regula-
ns for militia, pre-
ribed uniforms like
ose of the Federal
my, with state but-
ns and other devices.
is Virginian is wear-
g a uniform nearly
entical to the Federal
rsion, but with the
ge 'VA' within a
eath on his 'Hardee'
t and Virginia but-
ns. The specific unit
signation is
known.

Above: A group portrait of the officers of the West Augusta Guard, a militia company from the Shenandoah Valley of Virginia. These men wear the dark blue uniforms copied from the Federal army as prescribed in Virginia militia regulations. The West Augusta Guard later became a company in the 5th Virginia Infantry of the Stonewall Brigade. (CV)

Left: This young man, a student at John B. Cary's Hampton Military Academy in Virginia, wears a uniform that reflects strong Federal influence. Given the close proximity of the Federal garrison at Fort Monroe, less than two miles away, and the state regulations prescribing a uniform for state militia like that for the Federal army, this uniform was in keeping with pre-war Virginia militia practice. (Syms-Eaton Museum, Hampton, Virginia)

Right: This Virginian, a member of the Petersburg Riflemen, wears a uniform that vaguely copies the Federal form, but has its own idiosyncrasies, such as gold trim on the collar and cuffs, and a French-style kepi.

Left: The 1st Virginia Volunteers was one of the premier volunteer militia organizations in the South. Part of the reason was the regimental band, with its resplendent drum major, C.R.M. Pohle. Here he poses in full dress uniform just before the beginning of the war. (MOC)

Right: The 1st Virginia included a howitzer company in its organization. Here Private John Werth is seen in the company's uniform; gray jacket, trousers and forage cap, waistbelt with Virginia plate and light artillery saber. Once the war started, the howitzers quickly expanded to three companies, seeing service throughout the Virginia campaigns. (MOC)

ght: Private Robert Harper Carroll of the
ryland Guard. This company was formed in
ltimore City in 1859-60 as a part of the 53rd
giment Maryland Militia. They adopted a
uave uniform in response to the craze for the
ench style. When the war came, the majority
the members went south, but there is little
idence that the uniform followed. Most of the
mpany initially were part of the 21st Virginia
antry.

low: These men, probably members of the 1st
abama Volunteers, were photographed in May,
61 in one of the batteries facing Fort Pickens,
orida. They are prime examples of the early
ar commutation system; they have provided
eir own uniforms or clothing. Their apparent
ck of uniformity is the result of most of the
en having shed their coats, revealing a variety
shirt styles, and a variance in hat styles.
owever, the two officers (one in the rear center
th the light hat, the other in front wearing a
ard) both have civilian frock coats and wear
vords, while the soldier in front in the dark
ock coat may be wearing the company's nor-
al uniform. Those who are armed as infantry
ve oval plates on the waistbelts and round
ates on the shoulder belts. (NA)

Mississippi and Georgia, in prescribing uniform regulations, created a substitute for the eagle, a U.S. symbol, for the rank of colonel. Georgia prescribed a 'silver embroidered Phoenix rising from flame...' This photograph of Colonel Carnot Posey of the 16th Mississippi Infantry shows the Mississippi version, a gold crescent on the shoulder strap. (MOC)

Above: This photograph by J. D. Edwards, taken in May 1861, shows the camp of the Louisville Blues, a company of the 1st Alabama Volunteers. There appears to be little uniformity here, but that is primarily because the men are in their shirt sleeves. Once they put on their dark blue frock coats, like the one man seated, their appearance would be improved considerably. Even at this stage of the war, however, the casual look and the ubiquitous slouch hat are already in evidence.

Left: Mississippi regulations prescribed a hat turned up on three sides. This soldier is probably a Mississippian, although some Louisiana troops also followed the same practice.

Above: The 9th Mississippi Infantry had been enlisted only a few weeks when this photograph was made at Pensacola, Florida. One man sports a fireman's shirt bearing the number 4, and some of the men wear their hair closely cut, a style that was very popular in the early months of the war in the deep South.

Below: These men, members of Company B, 9th Mississippi Infantry, reflect Mississippi's practice of supplying its troops with arms, accouterments and uniform buttons, but not clothing. They were expected to follow state regulations in the manufacture of the uniforms, but there was great variet in the execution. These men show little uniformity except for the Mississippi rifles, accouterments, and light gray hats Two of the men wear checkered pants, but the others display a variety of gray or other light-colored clothing. (LC)

Opposite page: This sergeant of the Crescent City Rifles, a New Orleans company, is fully equipped in a gray service uniform with white canvas leggings. He carries full accouterments, including a knapsack and tin canteen, and is armed with a U.S. Model 1842 musket. (MOC)

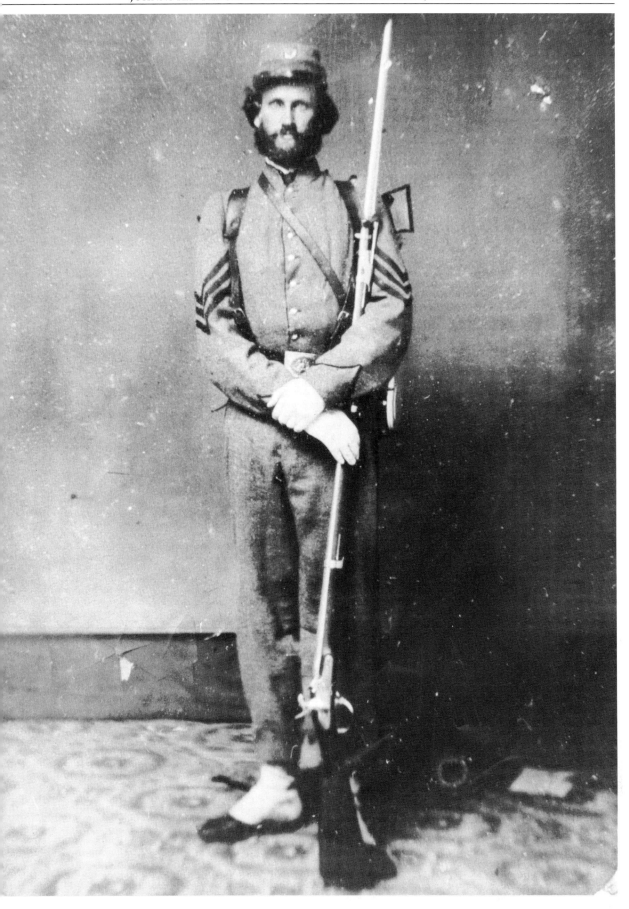

Left: Members of the 5th Company, Washington Artillery of New Orleans in their camp near the city in early 1862. This was one of the élite companies of New Orleans, and the men purchased their own uniforms. They wore gray jackets and trousers with red trim and carried their accouterments on white buff belts. (MOC)

Left: This Louisiana volunteer would be unidentifiable were it not for his state belt plate. Like Mississippi Louisiana generally supplied its troops only with arms and accouterments. Uniform designs were left up to individual companies.

bove: Private J. W. Noyes of the Orleans Cadets, a company Dreux's Louisiana Battalion, poses in Richmond in the ummer of 1861. This company already had been in service ome months when this photo was taken; photographs ken in Pensacola in May showed the men in the expected hirt sleeves. The trim on this frock coat is probably black.

bove right: This is an example where even early in the war, nits did not conform to regulations. This individual, Private

Albert Hall, served in the 1st Georgia Regular Infantry, but the uniform bears no resemblance to the published regulations for that regiment. According to the state regulations, he should have been wearing a single-breasted cadet gray frock coat trimmed in black with the regimental number on the collar, gray trousers and a black felt hat. The uniform here most closely resembles that of the Clinch Rifles. It is possible that the photo is misidentified. (MOC)

Left: This scene shows the Clinch Rifles, Company A of the 5th Georgia Infantry, who wore dark blue frock coats, kepis and sky-blue trousers, and carried Mississippi rifles. Here, the men have shed their coats. The caps bear an uncanny resemblance to that worn by Private Hall of the 1st Georgia Regulars.

Right: This unknown Georgian wears a light jacket possibly of cotton, and trimmed with tape. He wears an applied star on his belt plate and his accouterment belts may be of webbing. His bowie knife is Georgia made and provides the basic identification of his state affiliation.

Left: Sergeant Benjamin Barton, 8th Georgia Volunteers, wears a gray single-breasted frock coat which may be unfinished, because it has only three buttons in place. He wears a Federal-type forage cap in dark blue or black with undecipherable insignia on the top. His trousers may be sky-blue. (United Daughters of the Confederacy collection, Austin, TX)

Right: This photograph of Private Peter Jones of the 12th Virginia Infantry is interesting in that Jones wears the North Carolina State Troop issue sack coat. This is one example North Carolina supplying clothing to the troops of other states.

Above: The commutation system allowed practically any kind of clothing to be used, including civilian. Here Private F. A. Taulman, Co. G, 32nd Texas Dismounted Cavalry, poses in civilian clothes but carries saber, saber belt and Remington revolver. (CV)

Right: This ambrotype shows a Confederate wearing the North Carolina state issue sack coat. It has six North Carolina buttons, and the dark shoulder straps indicating infantry. The soldier is unidentified.

Left: Even in North Carolina, where troops generally were uniformed by state regulations, there were those companies that sported their own uniforms. These two men wear the so-called 'battle shirt', gray trousers and light-colored hats with the sides pinned up with buttons. Outrageous headgear was the craze with some volunteers, and one of these men has attached a large bag with a tassel – somewhat resembling the Phrygian cap – to his hat. (GHM

Right: Tennessee volunteers showed as much variety in their uniforms as most Southerners, though there was still a decided preference for dark blue. Robert B. Hurt, Jr., who became the adjutant of the 55th Tennessee, wears what is probably a dark blue frock coat, with light-colored trim and a seven-button front. A Federal Model 1851 sword belt plate closes his patent leather sword belt. His musket is an 1855 Harpers Ferry rifle, his revolver a Colt, and his knife probably an English import. (MOC)

Right: In early 1862, the North Carolina sack coat began to be reduced to a jacket. This photograph shows one of the early versions of that change. The garment retains the falling collar and dark shoulder straps, with a seven-button front, but now is shortened to waist length. (GHM)

Left: Two officers of the 1st Tennessee Volunteers (Turney's) Captain N. C. Davis on the left and Lieutenant Sugg, display the dark blue frock coats prevalent among some Tennessee troops. Captain Davis wears a U.S. 1858-style black hat, while his lieutenant sports a kepi. (CV)

bove: Some Virginia companies, particularly after the visit
the 7th New York to Richmond in the late 1850s, adopted
ay like the New York unit. This Virginian, possibly from
exandria, wears a gray frock coat with black trim, white
oss belts and gray kepi.

p right: This young private of the Old Dominion Rifles, a
mpany from Norfolk, Virginia, wears a gray jacket of
usual design. It may be a *chasseur* pattern, with short
irts. It has dark (probably black) wings on the shoulders
d corded cuff trim. His shako and overcoat are displayed,
is his rifle, a U.S. Model 1855. The Old Dominion Rifles
rved in the 6th Virginia Volunteers.

ght: Drummer Charles E. Mosby of the Elliott Grays,
mpany I of the 6th Virginia Volunteers. Mosby wears a
ple-breasted gray jacket, dark trousers, canvas leggings
d an unusual tasseled cap. His waistbelt is of white web-
ng, extensively issued by Virginia to its troops for accouter-
ent belts. As a drummer, Mosby probably was uniformed in
distinct manner. He may have been the only individual in
e army wearing this particular combination. (CV)

Above: Three members of the Sussex Light Dragoons, which became a company in the 13th Virginia Cavalry. Another photograph of a member of this company, plus a pre-war description, indicates that the unit normally wore dark blue frock coats with yellow trim. (MOC)

Right: This soldier is from one of several Lynchburg, Virginia companies that adopted similar uniforms, with the so-called 'battle shirt' as an upper garment. The term 'battle shirt' is modern, and has been used to describe the variously trimmed overshirts adopted by companies that (presumably) could not afford jackets or frock coats. This man is probably a member of the 11th Virginia Infantry.

Left: A member of the 11th Virginia, Sergeant Marion Seay of Company E, wears another version of the overshirt, this one trimmed vertically down the front, on the collar and the cuffs. While it would be incorrect to call the overshirt a true 'uniform', the 11th Virginia did attain some uniformity from its companies being dressed similarly. (CV)

Left: Captain Thoma B. Horton of Compar B, 11th Virginia, wea ing a shirt quite simi lar to that of the unknown member of this regiment. Although it is possib that both men were i the same company, the headgear is quite different and the col ors of the shirt are reversed. Unlike the soldier who wears a light shirt with dark plastron, Captain Horton wears a dark shirt with a lighter plastron. His gray ke is clearly much lighte than the shirt. (MOC)

ght: Another unknown Confederate, this quartermas-r sergeant was photographed in Richmond, Virginia, dging from the table and chair seen in other pho-graphs taken there. The weapons indicate that he is obably a cavalryman.

Left: Unfortunately, over the years, the identifications of many Confederate portraits have been lost. Until further research or luck produces an identification, the men in these portraits are simply unknown Confederate soldiers. This individual is an example. His uniform provides no real clue to his identity, and the initials on his cap, 'SG', could apply to any of a number of Southern companies.

Left: An unknown member of the 18th Virginia Heavy Artillery, this man wears gray forage cap and frock coat with shoulder straps. He carries a patent water filter canteen. The photo appears to have been taken in cold weather, probably the winter of 1861–2.

Right: Confederate infantry officers, as illustrated in the published regulations. The short Austrian tunic, and the collar and sleeve rank devices, are quite obvious here.

Left: Again unidentified, this man's jacket bears a certain resemblance to those worn by some companies of the 3rd Alabama Volunteers. Unfortunately, none of the details are sufficiently clear to be sure whether there is a connection. It is a classic example of much of the problem with Confederate uniform research.

Right: Austrian rank devices did not change significantly for many years. This scheme, although dating from World War I, is substantially the same as in the 1860s, and clearly shows the relationship between the Austrian system and the one Nicola Marschall proposed for Confederate officers. Not only are the rank devices on the collar, as in the Confederate system, but the basic scheme of stars was copied almost identically by the Confederates in the first version proposed. (Austrian Army Museum)

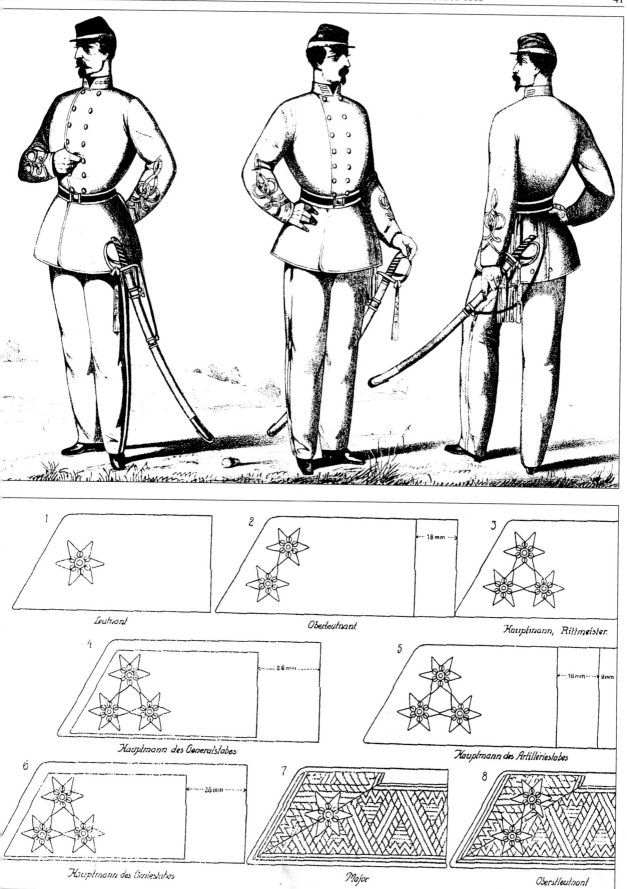

1. Leutnant

2. Oberleutnant

3. Hauptmann, Rittmeister.

4. Hauptmann des Generalstabes

5. Hauptmann des Artilleriestabes

6. Hauptmann des Geniestabes

7. Major

8. Oberstleutnant

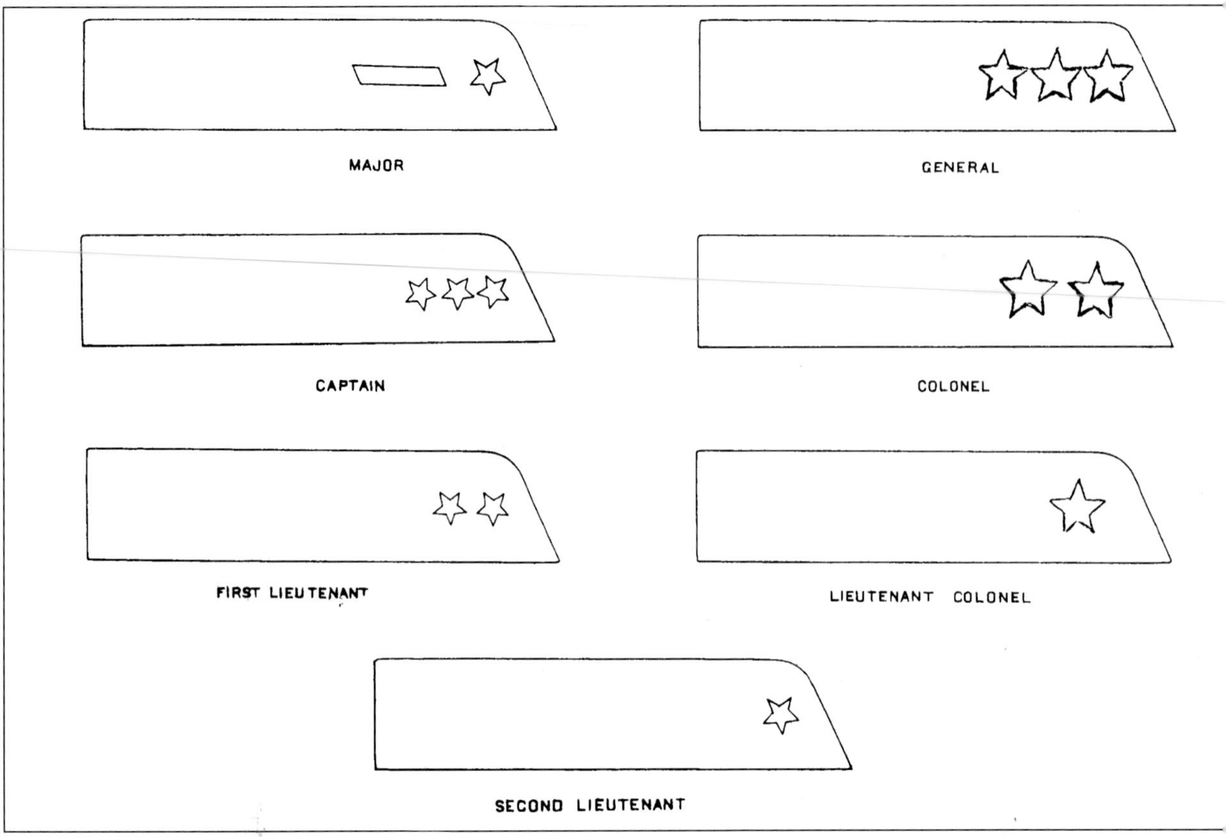

MAJOR

GENERAL

CAPTAIN

COLONEL

FIRST LIEUTENANT

LIEUTENANT COLONEL

SECOND LIEUTENANT

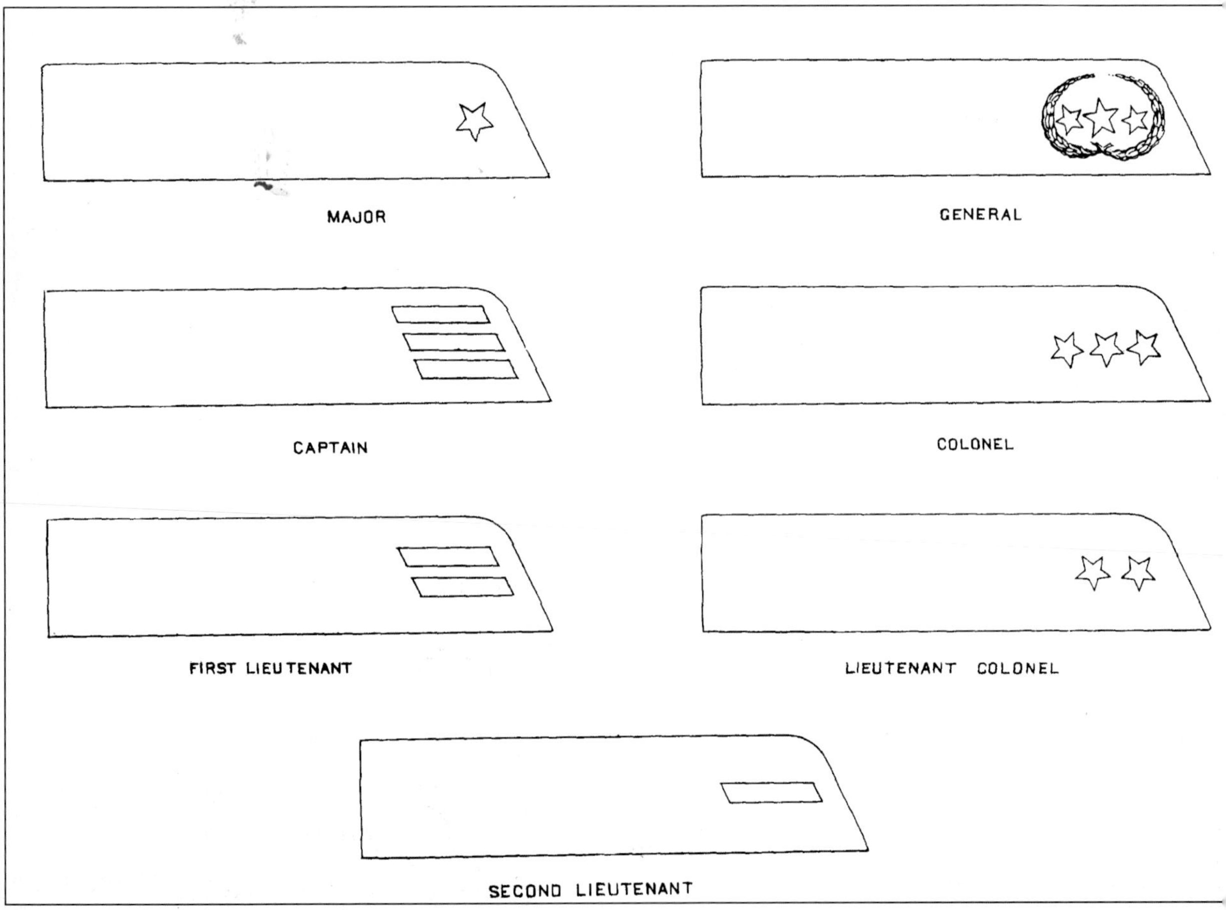

MAJOR

GENERAL

CAPTAIN

COLONEL

FIRST LIEUTENANT

LIEUTENANT COLONEL

SECOND LIEUTENANT

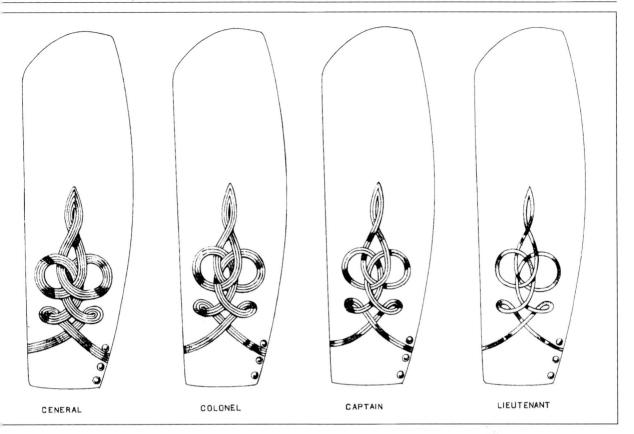

CENERAL   COLONEL   CAPTAIN   LIEUTENANT

pposite page, top: This scheme of officer rank insignia, scribed in an undated manuscript letter from about May 1861, ted that the uniform had been 'recently adopted' by the nfederate War Department. The scheme shown here admittedly interpretive; the letter describes the number and size of stars rge or small) but not their arrangement. They could have been ranged in the Austrian manner. The relationship between this d the Austrian system is quite clear. Also, in this system, the nk was on the collar only, in the Austrian manner. There was no eeve braid. (Author sketch)

pposite page, bottom: The published version of Confederate fficers' rank insignia retained the Austrian system of rank on the llars, as well as the stars for some ranks, but added bars for mpany officers and somewhat rearranged the insignia. This is e final version as used throughout the war.

bove: The Confederate system of sleeve braid, copied from the rench. In the final version of the uniform, as prescribed 6 June 861, this sleeve braid was worn with the collar devices.

ight: General James Longstreet and some members of his staff dopted the uniform as specified in the 1861 Regulations, includ-ng the short tunic. However, Moxley Sorrel, one of the staff, later emembered: ' ...The intention ... was to adopt the tunic like the hort, close fitting, handsome Austrian garment, but it went com-letely by default. The officers would none of it. They took to the miliar cut of frock coat with good length of tail. Longstreet and vo or three of us tried the tunic, but it was not popular...' .ee-Fendall House, Alexandria, VA)

Left: Confederate officers' uniforms generally conformed fairly closely to Confederate regulations. This second lieutenant wears the double-breasted frock coat with seven-button front and edge piping called for in the regulations, with the distinctive Confederate collar insignia and sleeve braid. His sword is English, and his belt is that of an enlisted man, with an oval CS plate. (GHM)

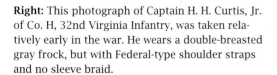

Right: This photograph of Captain H. H. Curtis, Jr. of Co. H, 32nd Virginia Infantry, was taken relatively early in the war. He wears a double-breasted gray frock, but with Federal-type shoulder straps and no sleeve braid.

above: This officer also wears the frock coat, but with an
[in]teresting braid scheme favored by some, particularly in the
[w]estern theater. This was a row of gold braid running up the
[sl]eve back-seam to about the elbow, where it usually ended
in a trefoil shape. The braid was normally trimmed, as in
this case, with numerous small ball buttons running up the
sleeve. The influence was French. (GHM)

Left: Some Confederate officers wore jackets like the men. Indeed, a general order from 1862 encouraged them to adopt enlisted dress in order to avoid casualties. This officer, Reuben Wilson of the 1st North Carolina Sharpshooters, wears a jacket with sleeve braid and 1st Lieutenant's bars on the collar. (GHM)

Below: An unidentified officer wearing a tailor-made but very plain jacket, with only 2nd Lieutenant's bars on the collar. (GHM)

Opposite page, left: A. R. Waud, the English newspaper artist, drew this Confederate officer at the same time he drew the bugler on page 65. He wears the classic frock coat with the sleeve braid. He was probably an officer of the 1st Virginia cavalry, or possibly the 55th Georgia Infantry, which Waud also sketched. (LC)

Opposite page, right: Captain Tom Pope Hodges of the 41st Mississippi wearing a very light-colored jacket, apparently with only collar insignia, dark trousers, dark slouch hat and sword belt. This was a typical uniform in the field for many officers. (V)

Right: This print of Austrian Marine Infantry, published in 1854 in a book on the Austrian Army, clearly shows the short tunic of that country and the collar rank devices that influenced Nicola Marschall in his design of the Confederate uniform. Although he was specifically influenced by Austrian *jägers*, the differences from Marine infantry were minor. (Pettenkofer and Strassgechwandtner, *The Austrian Army*, Vienna, 1854)

Below: This image of an officer in the field was taken by a captured Yankee photographer near Nashville in 1863. Lieutenant W. C. D. Vaught of the 5th Company, Washington Artillery, wears an overcoat over his jacket, and a kepi with his rank braid. His weapon is a light artillery saber.

Opposite page, top: The official view of the Confederate enlisted infantryman, as shown in the 1861 Uniform Regulations. The illustrated version of the regulations, with plates by Blanton Duncan, was not available until the fall of 1861. The plate shows the Austrian influence in the short, double-breasted tunics.

Opposite page, bottom: Confederate non-commissioned officers wore the same chevrons as their Federal counterparts. This plate, from the regulations, illustrates company level NCO rank.

SERGEANT   PRIVATE   MUSICIAN

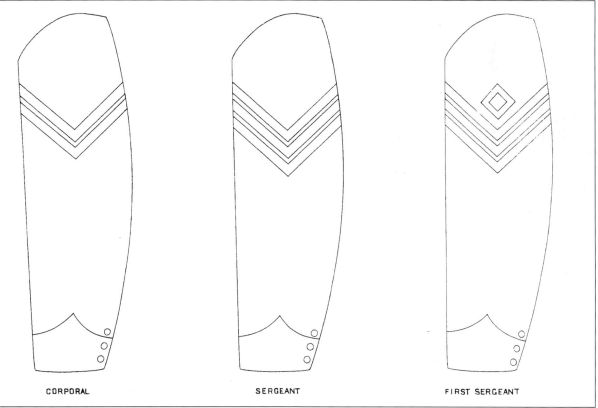

CORPORAL   SERGEANT   FIRST SERGEANT

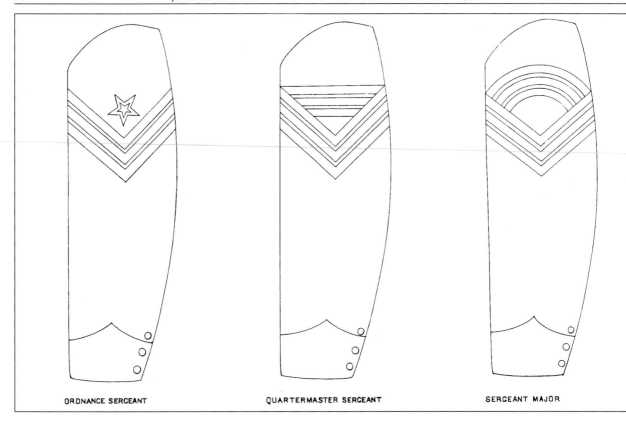

ORDNANCE SERGEANT   QUARTERMASTER SERGEANT   SERGEANT MAJOR

Above: Confederate non-commissioned staff chevrons.

Left: This Confederate enlisted man is wearing a double-breasted tunic or frock coat inspired by the Confederate regulations. However, the dark trim may be black, and could indicate that he is a Georgian or North Carolinian because both of those states prescribed that color for infantry.

ght: This unidenti-
d Confederate
illery sergeant's
form fits the regu-
ons very closely.
e only real anomaly
he light-colored
vrons. It probably
es from after 1862
en the regulation
nged the upper
ment to a frock
it. Unfortunately,
s man is unidenti-
d.

Left: A member of Crenshaw's Battery, an élite Richmond, Virginia organization. His jacket appears to be a Richmond Depot Type I, but is probably tailor-made, and may even be one of the uniforms that Captain Crenshaw, while serving in England as a contractor, purchased for the company. The kepi has a crossed cannon with 'C' and 'B' on either side.

Right: Sergeant William Crowder Owens, 9th Virginia Infantry, wearing another example of the Richmond Depot Type I jacket. Sergeant Owens was later killed at Gettysburg. (MOC)

Right: This photograph, taken 22 February 1862, shows Chief Trumpeter Charles H. Powell, Company F, 4th Virginia Cavalry, in one of the earliest known images of the Richmond Depot Type I jacket. It has the light color, trimming around the collar, shoulder straps and cuffs that characterize this style. (MOC)

ft: This jacket, a privately made copy of the *chmond Depot Type I, was worn by Sergeant C. N. Green of the 47th North Carolina State *oops. No actual Type I jackets made at the *chmond Clothing Bureau are known to sur-*ve. (North Carolina Museum of History)

ight: This back view shows the seam pattern of *e Richmond Depot Type II jacket. The belt *ops are just barely visible at the sides.

elow: This view shows the nine-button front, *oulder straps and top stitching around the *llar, down the front and around the cuffs that *istinguish the Richmond Depot Type II jacket.

elow right: Typical belt loop on the Richmond *epot Type II jacket.

ft: Sergeant John French White, Company K, 32nd Virginia
fantry, was photographed on 15 May 1863 wearing a new
chmond Type II jacket that was part of an issue to his regi-
ent received in April.

Above: First Sergeant Daniel Sheetz, Company K, 2nd
Virginia Infantry, Stonewall Brigade, wearing a Richmond
Type II jacket. Photographed in March 1864, Sergeant
Sheetz's jacket exhibits typical Richmond characteristics,
and in this case even the belt loops can be seen, but the uni-
form is a slight variant, having only a seven-button front.

Left: This photograph of an unidentified officer and enlisted man was taken by the Richmond firm of Rees and Company. The officer (a captain) wears the standard officer's frock coat and trousers with a slouch hat, while the enlisted man wears a rather baggy Richmond Type II jacket. His accouterments, featuring the so-called 'Georgia frame' buckle, are Confederate-made and his rifle musket is an Enfield.

Above: This jacket, worn by Private E. F. Barnes of the Richmond Howitzers when he surrendered at Appomattox, shows the nine-button front and plain shoulders of the Richmond Depot Type III jacket. (MOC)

Above right: Back view of the Barnes Richmond Depot Type III jacket. Note the lack of belt loops. (MOC)

Right: This Confederate, an unknown Virginian from Sperryville, wears the late-war Richmond Type III jacket minus the shoulder straps and belt loops of the earlier versions. Because his vest is made of the same material as the jacket, and vests were not issued by the Confederate Quartermaster's Department, the jacket is probably a private tailor's copy of the Richmond pattern.

This cadet gray wool jacket, worn by Private Garrett Gouge of the 58th North Carolina Infantry, was made by the Limerick, Ireland firm of Peter Tait and Company. It is piped in royal blue on the collar edge and shoulder straps. (GHM)

A rear view of the Tait pattern jacket, clearly showing the lack of a center back seam, a characteristic of this pattern. It is known that at least 4,400 jackets and pants from the Tait contract were imported into Wilmington, North Carolina by the steamer *Evelyn* in December 1864. (GHM)

Left: This butternut-gray wool jean jacket was worn by Private Elijah C. Woodward of the 9th Kentucky Infantry. It was probably a product of the depot at Columbus, Georgia. (Kentucky Military History Museum)

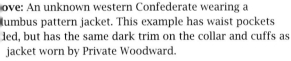

ove: An unknown western Confederate wearing a
umbus pattern jacket. This example has waist pockets
led, but has the same dark trim on the collar and cuffs as
jacket worn by Private Woodward.

ove right: Although Confederate regulations prescribed
rcoats, they were relatively scarce. Images of them in use
rare. This photo of Private Henry H. Kelly, 1st Virginia
talion, shows a pattern of overcoat known to have been
d in Virginia in the late 1850s by the 1st Virginia
unteers, and later in the Confederacy.

ght: This photograph of an unknown Confederate shows
same pattern overcoat as worn by Private Kelly. It is
aracterized by the large buttons and the tab under the
lar.

Left: This Confederate wears an overcoat that is similar to the previous type, but not identical. It has large, plain buttons, but no collar tab, and the material is somewhat different. Unfortunately, the man is unidentified.

Below: In the winter of 1861, members of the 1st Texas Infantry in camp at Dumphries, Virginia gather for a photograph. The men of this company, the St Rifles, wear jackets with a five-button front trimmed in dark braid, and dark blue forage caps with '1 TEXAS' and an 'SR' on either side of a star. One man wears an overcoat of the same pattern as worn by Private Kelly on page 63. Elements of the 1st Texas were supplied with quartermaster issue uniforms as early as November 1861.

Left: This drawing, done by A. R. Waud in the fall of 1862 while he was briefly in Confederate hands, shows the remains of the old regimental uniform of the 1st Virginia Cavalry still in use. (LC)

Right: Waud did this drawing about the same time as those of the 1st Virginia Cavalry. This infantry private, a member of the 55th Georgia Infantry, wears a coat very reminiscent of the Federal sack coat, and may in fact be wearing a captured uniform from the stocks at Harpers Ferry. (LC)

Left: This unknown Confederate infantryman, wearing full field equipment, exemplifies the devil-may-care attitude of much of the army. He wears a gray jacket with dark trim, has a dark stripe on his trousers and carries a captured Federal canteen, white cotton haversack and a rather small knapsack. His cartridge box still bears a plate and his musket is an altered flintlock.

Above: These men, photographed in May 1863 on the railroad bridge at Fredericksburg, are probably members of Barksdale's Mississippi Brigade, who were garrisoning the town at the time. The officer in his double-breasted frock coat is prominent. The majority of his men appear to have dark jackets and black hats. A number of them wear their cartridge boxes on shoulder belts, and brass buttons are obvious on most of the jackets. One man wears a rather baggy jacket and cap. (Mass MOLLUS)

Left: Conrad Wise Chapman, perhaps the Confederacy's best artist, produced this engraving of a camp of Wise's Brigade on Diascund Creek in early 1863. His depiction of Confederate uniforms shows the typical variety, but is especially important as one of the few true eye-witness sketches of Confederate troops in the field. Note the soldier wearing a blanket as an overcoat, while one of his comrades is in shirt sleeves. (Valentine Museum, Richmond, VA)

This classic photograph, perhaps the only true portrait of Confederate enlisted men in the field, is of three Confederates about to be sent to prison camp. It was taken about 15 July 1863, two weeks after the battle of Gettysburg. These men may have spent the previous two weeks procuring various Federal items to supplement their meager Confederate kit. All three carry Federal canteens, at least two (on right and left) have Federal haversacks, and the man on the left is wearing a Federal shirt. All apparently carry knapsacks, a far more common practice among Confederate infantry than legend allows. Their uniforms all appear to be Confederate. (LC)

Above: Photographs of bodies are among the best sources of information for Confederate field dress simply because there are so few photographs of live Confederates in the field. This man, killed in Devil's Den at Gettysburg, is interesting because he apparently went into battle wearing only a shirt. His cartridge box, which appears to be Confederate, is worn over his shoulder over the shirt. There is no indication that he wore a jacket. His trousers may be Federal, and the body has been looted, based on the turned-out trouser pocket. His shoes, however, are undisturbed. The musket is probably a photographer's prop, the same one seen in many of the Gettysburg views. (Mass MOLLUS)

Below: This is one of two photographs of the same man, probably a member of the 20th Georgia Infantry, showing him in his original position, down the slope of Devil's Den from where the second photograph was taken. He wears a lightweight single-breasted frock coat, with a six-button front and a large patch pocket on the left breast. His trousers appear to be of the same material, and his kepi lies on the ground near by. His shirt is white cotton. A small cotton haversack carried on a leather strap lies just under him along with a tin cup. The rifle musket was added by the photographer. (Mass MOLLUS)

bove: This view of the same body was taken after it had
∙en dragged a number of yards up the slope to the stone
∙ll area. The pocket and six-button front on the coat are
∙ite obvious, as is the shirt. While the trousers appear
∙mewhat lighter than the coat, the upper part of the body
∙ probably in shadow. The cartridge box and rifle musket
∙re evidently added by the photographer. (Mass MOLLUS)

Below: Taken in the Charleston, South Carolina defenses,
these members of the Palmetto Battery, South Carolina Light
Artillery, are relatively well uniformed and equipped. It is a
rare view of a Confederate unit from the mid-point of the
war. These men would have been supplied by the clothing
depot at Charleston. (Valentine Museum, Richmond, VA)

Below: Taken on the Alsop Farm at Spotsylvania on 20 May 1864, this dead Confederate was probably from Ramseur's North Carolina Brigade. He wears a gray wool jacket, with large brass buttons, and a paler-colored vest underneath, with small metal buttons. His trousers are of wool, and may be lighter in hue than the jacket. His black hat has a cord, and he carries an uncovered Federal bullseye canteen on a leather strap. The strap is interesting because it is split around the canteen itself, and attaches to the main strap with what appear to be the brass buttons used on Federal knapsacks. The jumble of straps around his right shoulder are apparently from a knap-sack. His cartridge box and cap pouch seem to be Confederate-made, and he wearing them on a waistbelt. The whit bundle under his head may be his haversack. A side view of the same body shows he is wearing shoes and t clothing appears to be in good condi-tion. (Mass MOLLUS)

Below: This row of bodies, taken at th Alsop Farm at Spotsylvania on 19 or 2 May 1864, is a particularly good view Confederate uniforms as worn by me bers of Ramseur's North Carolina Brigade. The man in front wears a ligh weight jacket, probably of jean or satinette, a military-style vest, a flann shirt and dark woolen trousers. His su pender tabs are clearly visible. The ma to his left also wears a lightweight jac et and trousers, and has tucked his trousers into his socks. The third bod has a dark gray jacket, a vest and ligh trousers. The fourth body is probably the same man as shown above, now stripped of his equipment. In all cases shoes and trousers appear to be in good condition. (Mass MOLLUS)

ove: The body of this soldier, also from the Alsop Farm,
s photographed twice, from the side and the front. He
ears a gray jacket of a somewhat thin material, with brass
ttons, spaced in such a way that it probably had an eight-
nine-button front. It has an inside pocket on the left side
ich has been pulled out. There is no indication of shoul-
r straps. He wears a dark shirt, and over the shirt a cum-
erbund or belly band, a non-issue item probably intended
ward off intestinal ailments. His trousers are wool, and
pear to be lighter in color than the jacket. His brogan
oes are in good condition. The checked item around his
leg may be a shirt. The large bundle under his head is a
Federal knapsack, and his Federal canteen, a smooth-sided
model, uncovered, is suspended from a thin leather strap
adjusted by a buckle. The haversack is Confederate, with a
large panel attached to the back side to prevent grease from
meat staining the clothes. He wears his cartridge box, which
may be Federal, on a Federal waistbelt with the U.S. plate
upside down. There is no cap pouch in evidence. The item
lying next to his left hand may be a cut-down Confederate
canteen used as a mess tin. (Mass MOLLUS)

Above: These men, captured at Cold Harbor on 3 June 1864, could be from several Confederate brigades. The group sitting down is of particular interest. Most of the men are wearing Richmond Depot Type II jackets, with shoulder straps and belt loops, and judging from the lay of the material, probably made of wool jean. The beegum hats, several of them with cords, also have a certain similarity. Among the group standing, a number of Federal-type, but gray, forage caps are in evidence, along with a few blue Federal ones. One man in the rear wears a light-colored hat with a Federal infantry insignia on the front. While there are a few frock coats in evidence, the vast majority of the men wear the jacket.

Below: Another detail from the same photograph. The man standing on the right, wearing the Richmond jacket with shoulder straps and the black hat, has a tooth-brush stuck in his button-hole – a practice commented on by a number of observers – and also carries what is probably a walking stick. He wears what appears to be a double-breasted vest. The man to his right and just behind has a tall beegum hat, but the same Richmond pattern jacket. He, too, wears a vest. The soldier standing with his side to the camera also has a Richmond jacket, this one with the belt loop showing. He wears his haversack under his jacket and appears to have either kepi or perhaps even a Confederate naval-pattern cap. He has turned his cuff up, showing the lighter underside of his wool jean trousers. The man next to him has a single-breasted frock coat, and darker trousers. His headgear is blurred, and may be either forage cap or even a slouch hat with the brim turned up on each side. The man to his right wears a Federal forage cap.

Opposite page top: Taken June 1864, the man in the center of this picture, with his hands on his hips, wears what appears to be a gray sack coat with a dark collar over his single-breasted vest. His hat sits at a rakish angle and his coat, vest and trousers all seem to be the same hue. The man to his right rear wears a Richmond pattern jacket, and the soldier sitting in front has a very light-colored uniform.

Opposite page, bottom: Taken at the White House in June 1864, the group sitting down, as well as some standing, wear a preponderance of Richmond Type II jackets, with shoulder straps and belt loops. Among the men in the rear, however, is a soldier wearing a very light-colored jacket, with a four- or five-button front, and a Federal forage cap. The men to his right and left both wear only shirts. The soldier two men to the right of the soldier in the light jacket has a double-breasted jacket or frock coat.

Above: This famous photograph shows Confederates captured in the Wilderness and at Spotsylvania in May 1864. The man looking at the camera, with the shelter half or coat draped over his arm, wears a heavy, light-colored jacket with a standing collar, and a black bowler-type hat. Other hat styles are in evidence. One soldier just behind the man in front has a knapsack, while another, standing in the shadow at the right, shows a row of brass buttons on his coat. None of these men have ragged knees to their trousers and all appear to be wearing shoes. (Mass MOLLUS)

Left: This detail of the above photograph shows haversacks, hat styles and blanket rolls a bit more clearly. A number of these men are wearing Federal forage caps. (Mass MOLLUS)

ght: Very few photographs actually illustrate ragged
nfederates. This one, however, of two members of
21st Virginia Infantry, taken in June 1864, does
ow ragged knees in one man's trousers. These men
ve shed their jackets, and the photo provides quite
lear view of the men's shirts, which appear to be
nnel – relatively rare late in the war.

low: This photograph of two men described as
bel Deserters' shows men who are in an advanced
te of deterioration. Indeed, their clothing is so
tched and ragged – and given the contrast between
se men and known photos of Confederates in the
d who are in much better condition – that this may
ssibly be a propaganda photograph. It is difficult to
alyze the uniforms, although the man on the left
pears to have a sack coat of Federal style, while the
n on the right has some kind of jacket. (Mass MOL-
S)

low right: These two men were killed at Petersburg
April 1865. The body in the foreground wears a
uble-breasted frock coat, and a vest over a light-
ored cotton shirt. His trousers are a lighter color
d his hat is black. The coat may indicate that he is
officer. The other man also has lighter-color
users than his upper garment, which is probably a
ket. Note that neither man has holes in the trousers
the shoes, an indication that the Petersburg troops
re reasonably well supplied, even late in the war.
ass MOLLUS)

Above: This photograph, taken at Fort Mahone, Petersburg in April 1865, shows a number of interesting details. The soldier is wearing one of the Irish-made Peter Tait contract jackets, distinguished by the double line of machine stitching on the right side, and the collar and shoulder straps of a darker broadcloth. The original photographer's label states the jacket was 'gray with red trim', indicating an artilleryman, yet this soldier wears a Federal infantry cartridge box on a shoulder strap. His canteen is an uncovered Federal bullseye with a split leather strap, and another view of the same body shows him with a large oilcloth haversack, and possibly a second cotton haversack, suspended from the narrow cotton straps here seen around his neck. His trousers are Confederate, probabl of a woolen jean, an his shoes also appea to be Confederate-made. The other pho tograph shows a bla slouch hat, with edg binding but without cord or crown ribbo lying next to the boc (Mass MOLLUS)

Left: This soldier, probably a member Godwin's North Carolina Brigade, is wearing the Type III Richmond Depot jac et, of heavy wool an without shoulder straps, a civilian ves underneath, and a c ton shirt. His trouse are of a material lighter in weight anc hue than the jacket. His small haversack protrudes from und his left elbow. (Mass MOLLUS)

ght: This is one of two pho-
graphs of the same body,
ken at Fort Mahone in April
65. The soldier wears a
hmond Depot Type II jack-
in heavy wool, with brass
ttons. The line of top
tching down the front of
e jacket is obvious. His
users also appear to be
ol and are a lighter hue.
e pocket configuration
y indicate that they are
deral, but this is not cer-
n. They have been tucked
o his socks. The shoes
pear to be Confederate,
t are so covered in mud
at the pattern is not dis-
rnible. (Mass MOLLUS)

ght: This photograph of
e same body as above
ows the jacket in slightly
ore detail. The inside
cing is obvious, as is the
bleached cotton lining. The
an wears no vest, and his
ite cotton shirt shows in
th views. The edge of a
oulder strap is visible just
der the jacket edge on the
t side. The buttons are
ite flat, and are probably
nfederate, possibly
fantry 'I' buttons. This jack-
has seen some service
ce the cuffs are quite worn
d getting ragged at the
ges. (Mass MOLLUS)

ght: This dead Confederate
ears a dark overcoat, distin-
ishable by the cape portion
ng on the ground on and
ar his left arm, and the
ndle near his head. The
de spacing of the buttons
so indicates that this is an
ercoat. The garment under
is either a jacket or a vest,
d the soldier wears a cot-
n shirt. A crumpled forage
p of a Federal pattern lies
ar his left foot. (Mass MOL-
JS)

Above: This photograph, though blurred, shows a narrow shoulder strap on the man's jacket, and two cuff buttons. The jacket material is quite wrinkled and is probably jean. (Mass MOLLUS)

Below: Confederates taking the oath of allegiance at the e? of the war in Richmond, 1865. This drawing by A. R. Waud an interesting study of Confederate knapsacks, haversacks and blanket rolls, and ways of wearing them. Note the use the walking stick – a practice probably more common than generally depicted. (LC)

INDEX

355.14 Jen
Jensen, Les.
Johnny Reb :

08/01/00 AGK-2882

DATE DUE